JESUS CHRIST

– Who is He?

JOHN MANOHAR RAJAN

INDIA • SINGAPORE • MALAYSIA

ISBN 979-8-88684-606-5

Contents

CHAPTER ONE

HE WAS LIKE NO OTHER

"Who is Jesus Christ?" Well, he is like no other.

Jesus Christ is the historical person who split history in two- B.C and A.D or BCE and CE as put nowadays. The miraculous nature of his birth, life, death and ressurection tells us that Jesus was no ordinary person. He was born and raised in a poor family. He had no servants but was called "The Lord", had no formal training in the scriptures, yet when he lived, he was addressed as "Teacher". All sixty-six books of the Holy Bible talk about him, but he did not write any of them.

He taught and ministered only for a little over three years, yet has more books written about him, than any other human! He held no prestigious posts in his life, nor had a wife or child. He did not even own a house nor travel much, but a maximum of two hundred and fifty miles from his village; didn't visit any esteemed cities of that time even. So humble was the life he lived.

It wasn't just his life that was humble, but so was his death. He was betrayed by one of his own, denied by another, deserted by his disciples, arrested like a thief and when he was crucified, he was crucified between two thieves and his garments were divided by lot. And finally, when he died, he was buried in another man's tomb.

Such was the humbleness of Jesus' birth, life, and death.

Yet, no army expedition or any invasion, no king or kingdom can match the impact this simple and humble life had on the history of man!

Jesus died, but he did not stay dead. He rose again to life- just as he said he would, proving beyond doubt, that he was not just an extraordinary person, but is Christ incarnate -the Son of God- just as he claimed.

CHAPTER TWO

ISRAEL'S POLITICAL SITUATION

As Jesus Christ is not a mythical person but a historical one, knowing the political situation he was born into, would provide a better understanding of the events that took place in his life.

Back then, the Romans who ruled over all the regions adjacent to the Mediterranean Sea - their empire extended from Europe to Asia and Africa. Israel was one of the nations along the Mediterranean Sea, was also under the rule of the Romans.

The Roman empire switched from being a republic to becoming a monarchy when the Roman senate appointed Agustus as the Caesar in the year 27 BC. Agustus ruled as a Caesar for 41 years right from 27 BC to 14 AD.

The Israelites were a fiercely independent nation and Jews were proud of their faith too. Therefore they naturally resented the foreign rule. And when the Romans tried to interfere with their religion, their resentment knew no bounds.

To pay for their lavish lifestyle, the Romans had the practice of imposing exorbitant taxes on the nations under their rule. This resulted in systematic exploitation of the population- leaving them in abject distress. This added fuel to the hatred of the Roman rulers among the Jews.

2.1 King Herod, administrator of Palestine

In 47 BC, Romans made a 25-year-old Herod the governor of Judea. Young Herod was an able administrator. He not only ably streamlined the tax collection of the region, but also brought security by controlling the bandits of the region. This remarkable success of young Herod earned him recognition from the Romans, and he was gradually entrusted with more responsibilities.

When a rebel named Antigonus II defeated a Rome appointed governor and took over Jerusalem, Herod demonstrated his military acumen by leading a large army to Jerusalem and taking back the city after a three-year war. This impressed the Romans so much that they granted Herod the privilege of using the title "King". Thus, Herod came to be called King Herod, although he was only a Roman governor for all practical purposes.

When Augustus won the power struggle in Rome and became the first Caesar, Herod managed to win his trust and entered his good books. This enabled him to consolidate his position further, and he continued as a king of Palestine, uninterrupted for a period of over forty years.

To gain the good will of the Jews, Herod expanded and rebuilt the temple of Solomon which the Jews dearly loved. The construction of the Temple took many years. This expanded version of the Temple that Herod invested so much was later referred to as Herod's Temple in history. This magnificent structure became a casualty when the Romans laid waste to Jerusalem in 70 A.D to put down a Jewish rebellion. The west wall - one of the foundations of Herod's Temple, still stands even today.

Although Herod was an able administrator, he was also a tyrant who would employ any means to remain in power and do anything to keep the region under his control. Any perceived threat to his position was dealt with iron fist. Even Herod's wives and children became victims of his paranoiac attitude. It was at the end of Herod's reign, and when Herod was nearly 70-year-old that Jesus Christ was born.

2.2 Expectations for the coming Messiah

Having been under the thumb of foreign kingdoms for five centuries, the independent natured Israelites yearned for a political savior.

Their pain under the current regime only escalated because their own leaders colluded with the alien oppressors for selfish reasons thereby were aiding the Romans in draining the nation's resources. This heightened the aspiration for a savior even more and they earnestly looked forward to someone who would free them of the clutches of the tyrant Romans.

Every single prophet of Israel had foretold the coming of a savior or "Messiah" - as they called him. It was told that, the Messiah would be from the lineage of David, the greatest king of Israel; the Messiah was expected to restore the throne of David.

It was into this socio-political situation, when every Israelite's heart ached for the Messiah, that Jesus was born.

CHAPTER THREE

BIRTH OF JESUS

The birth of Jesus was none like any other. It was accompanied by numerous miraculous happenings. It all started with the birth of John the Baptist to the old barren couple of Zacharias and Elizabeth,

Zacharias was a priest in the Temple of Jerusalem. He and his wife, Elizabeth lived in one of the cities of Judea in the hill country. This old couple was righteous in God's sight yet they were childless.

It was the custom of the Priest office to allot the job of burning the incense at the Temple. When it was his turn, Zacharias went into the Temple to perform his duty. As he stood offering burning incense, an angel of God named Gabriel appeared to him and told Zacharias that he would have a son and the boy was to be named 'John'.

Gabriel also told Zacharias that the baby would be filled with the Holy Ghost, even in his mother's womb and the child would be great in the sight of the Lord. Gabriel told him that John, would go before the Messiah, to prepare the people for the Lord, in spirit and power of Elijah (one of the most famous prophets of Israel) and that John will turn the hearts of the fathers to the children, and the disobedient to the wisdom of the just.

After his duties at the Temple were fulfilled, Zacharias returned home and just as the angel said, Elizabeth, his aged wife was soon pregnant! Everyone who learnt of this miraculous pregnancy was astounded.

Six months later, the same angel, Gabriel, appeared to a virgin named Mary in the town of Nazareth, Galilee. Mary was engaged to Joseph of the house of David. Gabriel told Mary that she would conceive and have a son and that she ought to name him Jesus. The angel said that Jesus "...shall be great and shall be called the Son of the Highest".

Since Mary was an unmarried virgin, and since it is impossible for a virgin to bear a child, Mary expressed her scepticism to angel Gabriel. Yet Isaiah, an ancient prophet had predicted this event nearly 700 years ago and had said that this will be a sign from the Lord Himself (Isaiah 7:14). This was truly a prophesy coming true.

To Mary's question, Gabriel answered that the Holy Ghost would come upon her and the power of the Highest, will overshadow her thus enabling her to conceive the child and said, "With God nothing is impossible". To show further proof Gabriel informed Mary that Elisabeth, her old and barren cousin is now pregnant with a child.

As soon as she heard the news about Elisabeth, Mary immediately surrendered to God's plan saying, "I am a handmaiden of the Lord. Be it unto me according to your word".

The news that Mary, a virgin, was pregnant, spread fast. Naturally, there were not many takers to Mary's claim that this was an act of the Holy Ghost. Her own fiancé, Joseph, was looking for ways to break off the engagement privately, as he did not want to embarrass her publicly. As he pondered on this, The Lord sent an angel to Joseph. The angel appeared to him in his dream and told him that everything that Mary was telling him was true and that he ought to be with her and when the baby was born, he ought to name him "Jesus". This was all Joseph needed and he decided to take Mary in. The couple then awaited together for the birth of the Lord, Jesus.

As these miraculous things were happening in Nazareth, Elisabeth had given birth to her child in Judah. The child was named John as the Lord had instructed. This John was later referred to as 'John the Baptist'. John's sole purpose and ministry was to introduce Jesus as the 'Messiah' to Israel.

As baby John turned six months old, Mary was nearing the final stage of her pregnancy.

At this time Augustus Caesar ordered a census in his kingdom. Now, this census was nothing like the census that we know. The census we know enables our governments to plan welfare programs for the citizens. But Caesar's census had only one purpose - to make the tax collection more effective. To be taxed, he decreed that the citizens of the whole Roman world should go to their respective own city. Since Joseph was of the lineage of David, he set out, from the city of Nazareth, Galilee to Bethlehem, Judaea, with his engaged wife, Mary. Because of the Roman census there was a huge influx of travelers and Joseph could not find any accommodation in the town. In this extremely unfavorable situation, Mary gave birth to her firstborn. On seeing the couple's dismal state, an innkeeper let them stay in his barn and Mary wrapped her firstborn in clothes and put him in a manger.

3.1 Visitors for the newborn

When Jesus was born, Mary and Joseph were in a town where they had no family or friends hence, not many knew of his birth. Since no one knew of Jesus' birth, Mary and Joseph did not expect any visitors either. But Jesus did have visitors and of course they were not the usual kind.

Angels from heaven appeared to the shepherds outside the town of Bethlehem who were tending their sheep. They informed them about the birth of savior the 'Christ' in Bethlehem. The shepherds were given a description of the baby - that they will find the child wrapped in cloth and laid in a manger. The astounded shepherds wasted no time. They immediately set out to visit the newborn king.

Sure enough they found the child as told by the angel. Joseph and Mary were pleasantly surprised to have these unexpected visitors. Later as the shepherds went their way, they told everyone what had happened, and what the angel had said about the child. All the people who heard them were equally surprised.

3.2 Bethlehem to Nazareth via Jerusalem

After the birth of the child, Mary and Joseph circumcised him on his eighth day as per the Law of Moses and named the child "Jesus" as they were told by Gabriel. The Law of Moses specifies that a woman who had given birth to a male child has to have 40 days of purifying (Lev. 12:1-8). When Mary's days of purification were over, the couple took the child to the Temple in Jerusalem to offer the sacrifices as per the custom of the Law.

Mary and Joseph had yet another surprise visitor at the Temple. Simeon, a just and devout old man, was waiting to greet them. The Lord God had revealed to Simeon that he should not see death before he had seen the Lord's Christ. Now on the day that Jesus was brought to the Temple, Simeon had been guided there by the Spirit of the Lord.

Simeon took the child in His arms and praised God. He then said, "Lord you now let your servant depart in peace, for my eyes have seen thy salvation". While handing the baby back to its mother, Simeon said a couple of things about the future ministry of the child and added that a sword shall pierce through Mary's heart -signifying the suffering she will endure in the end.

Another very old prophetess named Anna also came along as Simeon was talking with Mary and Joseph. She began praising the Lord and proclaimed to all the others around them about the child.

Mary and Joseph then offered the sacrifices that they had brought and returned to the town of Nazareth in the province of Galilee, but the surprises were far from over.

3.3 Arrival of the Magi

When Jesus was born as a baby in Bethlehem, Judaea, the wise men in the East who specialized in reading the stars, observed a new star - the one that told them that the king of Jews was born. Since Herod the Great was the king over the

Jews at that time, the wise men called Magi assumed that the baby must be born in Herod's palace.

These wise men then set out to Judea from the East so they could visit and worship the newborn King. They knocked on Herod's door and explained why they were there and instead of answers, their request was answered with very surprised looks from everyone in the palace including Herod.

Herod was a tyrant who did not tolerate threats and was known for his zealous defense of his political position. So when the wise men came with the news that a king of Jews was born, Herod lost his temper and the atmosphere in the palace changed extremely quickly. As everyone was aware of Herod's capacity to react to such a threat, the whole capital trembled.

Herod knew that the Jews had been waiting for a savior for centuries. He therefore called the High Priests and the scribes and enquired with them the place where the savior was expected to be born.

To this, the religious leaders pointed to a 700-year-old prophesy by prophet Micah, which says that the savior will come from Bethlehem (Micah 5:2). After that confirmation, Herod enquired with the visiting wise men the timing of the sighting of the stars.

Herod wanted to kill the newborn king but did not want to be obvious about it. Hence he pretended to be interested in the whereabouts of the newborn king saying that he wanted to pay his respects too and asked the Magi to help him with this. The unsuspecting wise men agreed and left the palace.

They were pleasantly surprised to see the same star that was sighted in the East. This star led them from the palace to the actual place where the baby was. When they saw the young child, the wise men's joy knew no bounds. They fell down and worshipped the young child and offered to him gifts of gold, frankincense and myrrh.

The wise men did not know about the sinister plans of Herod and were about to return to Herod's palace to give the details of the child's whereabouts, but they were warned to not return to the palace but go back to their country using a different path by an angel and the Magi did so. The angel then warned Joseph to flee to Egypt with the child and its mother, to escape Herod's insanity. Joseph did so that same night and remained there until further instructions.

It did not take long for Herod to realize that he had been let down by the Magi and he was furious. So, he decided to deal with the matter in his own style. Herod ordered the killing of all boy children below the age of two in and around the town of Bethlehem. This attempt by Herod to kill Jesus, was the first attempt among very many later to kill him.

3.4 Return to Nazareth from Egypt

Herod the Great's life came to an end soon after at the age of seventy. After his death the Romans divided Herod's kingdom of Palestine into four, and appointed four Tetrarchs to govern over them. None of Herod's sons were given the privilege of calling themselves 'king' as Herod the Great did. Herod's son Archelaus was given the province of Judaea to govern.

When Herod died, an angel told Joseph that it was safe to return to Israel. But since Herod's son was in power Judaea, Joseph took an alternate route to purposefully avoid Jerusalem on the way back to Nazareth.

CHAPTER FOUR

BEGINNING OF JESUS' MINISTRY

4.1 Baptism of Jesus

Augustus Caesar, who was the ruler when Jesus was born, died in the year 14 AD. He was succeeded by Tiberius Caesar. And in the 15th year of Tiberius Caesar (29 AD), John, the son of Zacharias, began his ministry.

John came to the wilderness of Judaea preaching, "Repent for the kingdom of God is at hand." Soon his ministry became popular, and people came from Jerusalem, all of Judaea, and all the region around Jordan to listen to him. John not only preached his sermons, but he also baptized those who submitted themselves to his teachings.

Ceremonial bathing was one of the traditions of the Jews. According to the law of Moses, anyone who is made impure by a corpse will have to purify themselves by taking a ceremonial bath. Based on this tradition, John taught them to purify oneself who had become impure in the sight of God by sin, through repentance and water baptism. Since John advocated water baptism, he was called 'John the Baptist'. John used the river Jordan river to baptize.

River Jordan originates 100 kms North of the Sea of Galilee and enters its northern side. The river Jordan then resumes its flow from the southern end of the Sea of Galilee and runs nearly 125 kms (total length of the Jordan river is 251 kms) to empty into the Dead Sea which is 1385 ft below the sea level. It was in the second phase of the Jordan river-area near the wilderness of Judaea, that John the Baptist was ministering.

Preaching and baptizing were not the primary objective of John's ministry. The primary objective was to announce the coming of the Messiah and to identify him to the Jews.

Since John was preaching the repentance from sin, people began to doubt if he himself was the expected Messiah. When questioned about it, John unequivocally denied it, saying the one who is going to come after him was much greater than himself and that he did not consider himself to be fit to carry even his sandals. John said that he was baptizing people with water; the Messiah who comes after him will baptize people with the Holy Ghost and fire.

As John was thus ministering in the wilderness of Judaea near the Jordan, Jesus who was now 30 years of age came down from Nazareth to the spot where John was ministering. As people waited in the line to be baptized, Jesus also joined the queue. When John saw Jesus, he immediately recognized him and attempted to prevent him from being baptized by saying that he should be the one to be baptized by Jesus. But since Jesus insisted, John baptized him.

When Jesus came out of the water after his baptism, two miraculous things happened. First, as soon as he stepped on the land, he saw a vision of the Spirit of God descending from heaven like a dove and alighting upon him. Second, a voice came from heaven saying, "Here is my beloved Son, in whom I am pleased."

4.2 The temptation and the fasting

Soon after his baptism Jesus was led by the Holy Spirit into the wilderness to be tempted by the devil. There he was tested for forty days and forty nights straight. During those days Jesus did not eat or drink anything, he fasted.

After those forty days, Jesus was hungry. The tempter (the devil) came to him and said that he was, indeed, the Son of God, he could command the stones to become bread. Jesus refused to give in to the temptation by saying that, "Man shall not live by bread alone but by every word that proceeds from the mouth of God."

Next, the devil took Jesus up to an exceedingly high mountain and showed him all the kingdoms of the world and their glory. And he said to him that if he fell down and worshiped him, he would give all those things to him. To this Jesus retorted saying, "It is written you shall worship the Lord your God and Him alone you shall serve."

Now, for the last time the devil took Jesus to Jerusalem and set him on the pinnacle of the temple and enticed him by quoting a verse from the scriptures himself. He said, "If you are the Son of God, throw yourself down. For it is written, "He shall give his angels charge over you, and they shall bear you up in their hands." To this temptation, Jesus replied again with a verse from the scripture saying, "It is written you shall not tempt the Lord your God."

With this the devil departed from him until an opportune time.

4.3 "Behold the Lamb of God"

After his forty days' temptation, Jesus returned to the spot where John was ministering. When John saw Jesus, He proclaimed to those around him, "Behold! the Lamb of God, who takes away the sin of the world. This is he who baptizes with the Holy Spirit!"

Until then, John had spoken of Christ as, "He who is coming after me," but now, he identified Jesus to the crowd as, "This is he, whom I said".

And again the next day when John was in company of two of his disciples, he happened to see Jesus. Once again John introduced Jesus as 'the Lamb of God'. When the two disciples who were with John heard this, they went with Jesus and stayed the night with him. One of them was Andrew,

Simon Peter's brother.

The next day Andrew told his brother Simon that he had found the Messiah. He brought Simon to Jesus - who named him Peter. Jesus found Philip and called him to follow him. Philip, who was from the Galilean city of Bethsaida, brought Nathanael, who was also from the same city to Jesus telling him that he had found the Messiah and he was Jesus of Nazareth.

These five people became the initial followers of Jesus Christ.

CHAPTER FIVE

THE MIRACLES OF JESUS

Jesus started his ministry at the age of thirty and ministered for a little more than three years. During this period, he performed many supernatural miracles. These miracles flabbergasted both the people who witnessed them, and those who heard of them. Never had they seen such happenings in their lives. As a result, the people of Israel watched and listened to Jesus with amazement.

5.1 First miracle at Cana

On the third day after Peter, Andrew, Philip, Nathanael had started to follow Jesus, they attended a wedding feast in Cana, Galilee. Cana was 9 kms Northeast of Jesus' native town Nazareth. Jesus and His disciples were invited to the feast. Jesus' mother Mary was at the wedding too. In those days, a Jewish wedding feast would last up to seven days. And at this wedding feast, there was a shortage of wine. Mary, the mother of Jesus, informed him of the shortage.

Jesus asked the servants to fill six large jars with water. He then asked the water to be served in the feast. When served, this plain water became one of the finest wines! This wine was so much tastier than the one served earlier that the guests were surprised.

5.2 Second miracle also at Cana

The son of a nobleman in Cana was sick, and he needed help. Jesus was in town after a brief trip to Jerusalem. When the noble man came to know of Jesus' return, he went and pleaded with Jesus to come and heal his son. Instead of acceding to his demand, Jesus just stayed put and told the noble man to go home and that his son was healed. Trusting Jesus' words, the noble man got home. He was pleasantly surprised to see his son well again. He then inquired about the hour the boy got better. They said, "Yesterday at the seventh hour" and the father knew that it was the exact hour when Jesus said that his son was healed. He and his entire household since then, became believers of Christ.

5.3 The miracle that astonished Peter

Jesus moved his ministry from Judaea to Galilee. He skipped his native town of Nazareth and started his ministry with Capernaum. Capernaum was home to Peter and his family, who were all fishermen by profession. Though Peter's native was Bethsaida, they lived in Capernaum so did his friends James and John, who were fishermen too. While in Capernaum, Jesus stayed at Peter's house and carried on his ministry.

Once, Peter and Andrew along with James and John returned empty handed, from a nightlong fishing trip. As they were washing their nets by the side of their boats, Jesus came by. Jesus borrowed Peter's boat for some time to preach for those who had gathered there and after finishing his sermon, he asked Peter to launch his boat into the deep and let down their nets for a catch. To this Peter replied, "Master we have toiled all night and caught nothing; nevertheless at your word I will let down the net". He did so, not with much hope but just out of respect.

But to his great amazement, the net was filled with fishes. They caught such a great number of fishes that their nets almost ripped! They had to signal their partners to come and help them. The catch was such that both the boats were filled with fish. This miracle astonished Peter so much that when they came to the land he said to Jesus, "Depart from me Lord for I am a sinful man" and his partners said the same.

But Jesus replied, "Follow me, and I will make you fishers of men." All four of them immediately left everything they had and followed Jesus.

When they arrived at Peter's house, they found Peter's mother-in-law down with fever. Jesus gave her a hand, the fever left, and she was healed. That evening a large crowd came to Peter's house seeking miraculous cure from Jesus.

All those who were sick with any disease were brought to Jesus. Jesus laid his hands on every one of them and healed them. People possessed by demons were healed. Sick including deaf, dumb, and even lepers were cured by Jesus. Never had miracles of this magnitude had ever been witnessed. As a result the popularity of Jesus gained rapidly, his name and fame began to spread far and wide.

5.4 In every village and every city

Although Jesus had his miracle performing powerful ministry centered in Capernaum, he did not limit himself to that city alone. He traveled to every city and every village in Israel, preaching and healing all the people who came to him. People from every direction began to come to follow him, basically to hear him preach and to be delivered miraculously of their afflictions. There was always a huge crowd of people milling around him; so much so that Jesus and his disciple did not have time even to eat or rest. Jesus thus traveled across the provinces of Galilee, Decapolis, Naphtali, Samaria, and Judaea preaching and spreading God's message.

The Jewish religious leaders in Jerusalem sent a team to inquire about the nature of Jesus' ministry. This team met up with Jesus in Capernaum. As they sat watching Jesus preach, there rose an opportunity for Jesus, to show this team, who he really was. There came four men carrying one of their friends with his cot. This friend of theirs was stricken with paralysis. Finding no room to enter the house, they climbed the roof, removed the tiles, and lowered the paralyzed man before Jesus with his cot and all!

To declare to the team from Jerusalem, that he was no ordinary preacher but the Son of God himself, Jesus, instead of just healing the crippled man, said to him, "Son, be of good cheer; your sins are forgiven for you!"

These words of Jesus rattled the Scribes in the team. "How could an ordinary man say such a thing, when God alone could forgive sins?" they wondered and concluded, "This is blasphemy!"

Knowing their thoughts, Jesus asked them a very meaningful question. "Which is easier to say, 'Your sins are forgiven' or, 'Arise and walk'?" he asked. Naturally, the former was easy, as it cannot be verified. Saying the latter is of course complicated. Having asked this challenging question, for which the answer was obvious, Jesus said, "But, that you may know that the Son of Man has power on earth to forgive sins. . ." he turned to the paralyzed man in the cot and told him, "Arise! take up your bed, and go to your house!"

To the amazement of all those present, the crippled man rose and went to his house! Everyone marveled. The team from Jerusalem went back saying, "We have seen strange things today! We have never seen anything like this!" Jesus thus, unambiguously showed the Jewish spiritual leaders that far from being just another preacher, he was indeed the **Son of God who could forgive sins of man**.

Apart from miracles like this, Jesus brought even the dead people back to life. When the twelve-year-old daughter of Jairus, one of the rulers of a synagogue died, Jesus visited their house and brought the child back to life saying, "Little girl, I say to you arise!" Once when Jesus along with His disciples visited the town called Nain, they came across a funeral procession. The young man who had died was the only son to his widowed mother. Taking pity on the widowed mother, Jesus touched the coffin and said, "Young man I say to you, arise!" Barely were these words spoken, the dead man sat up and began to speak! Another time Lazarus, with whom

Jesus was friendly, died after an illness when Jesus was not in town. By the time Jesus reached their town of Bethany, it was four days since the funeral. Upon reaching Bethany, Jesus demanded the grave to be opened. He then called out, "Lazarus come forth!" The dead and buried Lazarus came out alive with his hands and legs still bound with grave clothes!

5.5 Miracles in Jerusalem too

To celebrate the Jewish festivals, Jesus used to travel from Capernaum in Galilee to Jerusalem in Judea. By this time Jesus had chosen 12 people out of his disciples to be his apostles. They are as below:

1. Simon whom he called Peter
2. His brother Andrew
3. James
4. His brother John
5. Philip
6. Bartholomew
7. Thomas
8. Matthew
9. James, son of Alpheus
10. Lebbeaus whose surname was Thaddaeus
11. Simon the Canaanite and,
12. Judas Iscariot, who betrayed him.

All through his regular journeys from Nazareth to Jerusalem, Jesus used to preach and minister to all the people in every city and village along the way.

Once in Jerusalem Jesus healed a sick man near the pool called Bethesda. To the person stricken with the disease for the past 38 years, Jesus just said, "Rise, take up your bed and walk." As soon as Jesus uttered these words, the sick man was instantaneously healed! And he did just as Jesus commanded-stood up and walked!

In another instance Jesus opened the eyes of a person born blind. This blind person used to sit at the Temple entrance and beg for alms. To this person born blind, Jesus spat on the ground and made clay out of the mud and saliva, put it on the blind man's eyes and commanded him to go to the pool of Siloam and wash it. When the blind man did so, his eyes were miraculously opened! The people around could not believe what happened. Many said he was the blind who had been begging; while others said he resembled that blind man that's all. But the healed blind man kept saying, "I am that blind man!" People who opposed brought his parents for questioning. But the parents without any hesitation affirmed that he indeed was the person who was blind and now could see!

Wherever Jesus went, he performed such mighty miracles which none could deny. To him, performing miracles seemed to be the norm. Even the incurable disease of leprosy was healed in an instant at Jesus' command. Once when a leper said to Jesus, "Lord, if you are willing you can make me clean." To this Jesus replied, "I am willing. Be cleansed" and immediately his leprosy was cleansed.

Another time when Jesus was passing by ten lepers cried out to him, "Jesus, master, have mercy on us!" Jesus told them to go and show themselves to the priest as if they had been cleaned. Trusting they did as they were told; and, on the way, all of them were cleaned!

5.6 Deliverance from evil spirits

Jesus not only healed people of their sickness but also delivered people from the possession of evil spirits. The devils trembled and shrieked at the sight of Jesus. Some of them even cried, "What have we to do with you Jesus, you Son of God? Have you come here to torment us before time?", Some acknowledged his position of authority saying, "I know who you are -The Holy one of God!".

Jesus always cast out the demons saying, "Be quiet and come out of him!" without giving them any chance to proclaim him. Jesus never entertained any praise or recognition from the mouth of the devils. He just commanded them with authority, and they fled screaming in terror!

Once Jesus and his disciples crossed the Sea of Galilee and landed in Gergesenes. There he was confronted by two men who were possessed with numerous devils and lived among the tombs. Once they saw Jesus, one of them screamed, "What have I to do with you, Jesus, son of the most High God? I implore you by God that you do not torment me!"

These two men were so exceedingly fierce that none could pass that way. They could not be bound by chains, as they pulled them apart and the shackles were broken into pieces, and neither could anyone tame them. And always by night and day, they were in the mountains and in the tombs crying out and cutting themselves with stones.

When Jesus asked these two what their name was, they replied, "Our name is Legion for we are many!" A legion is a Roman military contingent of 6000 men. To show that there were that many evil spirits in those men the devil used that name.

The devils begged Jesus earnestly that He may not drive them away from that country. A large herd of swine, about two thousands of them, were grazing nearby. The evil spirits asked Jesus' permission to go into them. When Jesus granted their wish, the spirits left the men and entered the herd of swine; the herd ran violently down the steep place and into the sea and drowned. The men delivered from the evil spirits immediately became men of right mind! Those who witnessed this event were just amazed.

Once, when he cast away an evil spirit, the person who was dumb till then, began to speak. Jesus also set free a woman who, because she was bound by the devil, was bent over, and could not stand upright in eighteen years.

5.7 Even nature obeyed Jesus!

The power and authority of Jesus did not stop with healing the sick and casting out the demons, he also did miracles that overruled nature. Once after preaching to a large audience,

Jesus expressed his desire to feed them all. But five loaves of bread and two fish were all they had. When Jesus blessed and distributed them to the crowd, the bread and the fish started to multiply. In the end not only were the crowd that consisted of five thousand men apart from women and children satisfied, but they also even had twelve baskets full of leftover fragments!

Another time when Jesus wanted to feed his listeners, they had only seven loaves of bread and few fish. This time again when Jesus blessed the bread and fish, they started to multiply! As a result, the crowd of four thousand men, besides women and children were satisfactorily fed. And again, as last time the leftover fragments filled seven baskets!

There were instances when the disciples were amazed to witness nature obeying Jesus' commands. Once when Jesus and His disciples were in a boat crossing the sea of Galilee, there arose a storm which threatened to fill the boat with water. Such storms were a common feature in that part of the world. Jesus was asleep at that time. Many of Jesus' disciples including Peter being fishermen by profession were quite capable of handling such exigencies. But since this situation proved too much for them, they had no option but to call upon Jesus. When Jesus was awakened, instead of being distressed with them over the situation, he just commanded the sea and the wind to calm down! And they did! Amazed by this, the disciples filled with fear and said, "Who can this be, that even the wind and the sea obey him!"

Soon after, a near similar situation arose. This time Jesus was not on the boat, he was on the shore praying alone. The disciples of Jesus were attempting to cross the sea of Galilee. The wind being against them proving their labor to row the boat, futile. As they were struggling at the oars, Jesus came walking on the water. At the sight of a person walking on the water, the disciples shrieked in terror crying, "It is a ghost!" But when they found out it was Jesus, they agreed to let him aboard the boat. Once Jesus boarded the boat, the wind ceased! At this miracle, those on the boat were astonished and they fell in front of him in worship saying, "Truly you are the Son of God!"

TEACHINGS OF JESUS

Jesus was not only performing miracles, but he also preached the message of salvation saying, "Repent, for the kingdom of God is at hand." The teachings of Jesus were radically different from the usual preachers. Although Jesus was not formally trained by the scriptures, the knowledge he commanded took people by surprise. Even at the tender age of twelve when Jesus visited the Temple in Jerusalem with his parents, he was found sitting among the teachers and everyone who heard him were amazed at his understanding and his answers.

Jesus gave importance to the inner self of man. For the outer self to be clean, first the inner self must be made clean, was his teaching. When the mouth of a man speaks everyone hears; but it is with fullness of the heart that the mouth speaks, said Jesus. To a society that put all its effort in ritualistic religious practices, Jesus explained that it is not what that goes into the mouth that defiles you; it is what comes out of it. Because, what comes out of the mouth comes from the heart. From the heart comes evil thoughts -murder, adultery, sexual immorality, theft, false testimony, and slander. These are the ones that defile a person.

To those who like to put on an outward show of piety or self-righteousness, Jesus reminded them that God sees the inner man; therefore, they ought to take effort to cleanse one's inner self. Jesus insisted on the heart of man rather than the outward actions because it is what the Lord God in Heaven sees.

God had made this plain to the Old Testament prophet Samuel. "Lord does not look at things that people look at. People look at outward appearance, but the Lord looks at the heart" said God to Samuel (1 Samuel 16:7).

Jesus' teachings were based on this truth. Hence, he said, "God who sees what is done in secret shall reward you openly."

Secondly, instead of giving importance to the rituals of the religion, Jesus gave more emphasis to heart felt love, mercy, and compassion. Jews in those times, gave more importance to the celebration of Temple festivals, tithes, and offerings. The standard of one's spirituality was usually measured in those terms. Jesus' teachings in such an environment was radically different.

For example, according to the Law of Moses, Saturday - the seventh day of the week must be considered as The Sabbath day. The Jews took this command a bit too seriously and considered that even doing a good thing on the day of Sabbath as a violation of the Law. This, exactly, was the attitude that Jesus objected to.

For the sake of keeping the Law, one cannot do away with mercy and kindness was Jesus' argument. To prove his point, Jesus never procrastinated his miracles of healing anyone on the account of The Sabbath. This action of kindness and mercy by Jesus on the day of Sabbath, was considered by the Jews as a violation of the Law. This attitudinal difference spawned seeds of enmity between them.

Jesus called the act of neglecting justice, mercy and faithfulness ascribed in the law and giving undue importance to other dictates of the law, such as tithes and festivals as, straining out a fly and swallowing a camel!

When we talk about the teachings of Jesus, both his sermon on the mount and his sermons of parables will need to be mentioned.

6.1 *The sermon on the mount*

The sermon on the mount is a very popular sermon of Jesus. This sermon of Jesus is often quoted by many notable personalities across the nations till today. Mahatma Gandhi, the father of India in particular, mentioned many parts of this sermon as his main motivator for the non-violent movement launched by him- that successfully freed the nation from the British clutches.

The sermon on the mount brought to the fore Jesus' distinctive style of teaching. In this sermon, Jesus quoted the general teachings and then what he had to say about that subject saying, "I tell you that...." They are as follows:

- Murder is prohibited generally. But Jesus said that being angry with one's brother without reason or calling them empty one or a fool also tantamount to murder.
- Adultery is forbidden generally but Jesus said that a mere lustful look at a woman is equal to committing adultery.
- In those days in Israel, it was accepted that it was right to divorce a wife by issuance of a certificate of divorce. But Jesus taught that except for the charge of adultery, divorce cannot be invoked. The one who divorces but for this charge, makes her a victim of adultery; and anyone who marries a woman who was divorced for the said charge, commits adultery himself.
- It was customary to swear an oath for a vow. Jesus forbids this system and exhorted people to just say yes when it is a yes and no when it is a no; anything beyond that comes from the evil one.
- Jesus also was against the culture of retaliation. Although it was taught to repay eye for an eye, tooth for a tooth. But Jesus asked his followers to turn the other cheek as well if one is slapped on one cheek; love their enemies; bless those who curse them; do good to those who hate them; pray for those who persecute them. Only then they will truly be called as the sons of the Father in heaven.

- To gain recognition in society, it was customary to advertise one's charitable deeds before men. But Jesus said, charity must be done in secret so that the left hand should not know what the right hand is doing! This was because the God in heaven sees in secret and rewards openly. For the same reason Jesus taught to pray or fast in secret.
- Since God of the Heaven was our Father, Jesus advised not to worry about what to eat, drink or wear. Because our Father in heaven knows our needs and will provide them.
- Jesus admonished the hypocrisy of finding fault with others when we ourselves are not perfect. He compared it to a person trying to remove a speck from his brother's eyes when there was a plank in one's own eyes!
- Do unto others what you wish to be done to you taught Jesus.

Thus, Jesus' approach to truth was diametrically different to other teachers.

6.2 The use of parables

The use of parables by Jesus is one of his unique styles of teaching. Many of his parables are popular far and wide even today. Let us see a few of them.

1. A shepherd who found a lost sheep

A man had one hundred sheep. One of them was lost. The shepherd's concern for the lost sheep was such that he left the ninety-nine sheep in the wilderness and went searching for it. He searched till he found it. When he came back, his joy was such that he called his friends and neighbors to rejoice with him for finding the lost sheep. Likewise, there will be more joy in heaven over one sinner who repents than over ninety-nine who need no repentance, Jesus taught. By saying this parable, Jesus showed how concerned is God the Father over the repentance of the one sinner.

2. The son who repented (The Prodigal son)

A man had two sons. The younger of the two demanded that the property be divided, and he be given his share. When the father did so, the younger son sold whatever that was his and left town to a distant land. There, he swindled his money in lavish and sinful ways. Soon famine set in, and this son found himself working as a swine feeder for survival. He finally realized what needed to be done and decided to go back to his father and beg for his forgiveness and plead with him to be taken by him back -at least as one of his servants.

With this objective, the younger son set out to go home. As he walked home, his father identified him while he was still far away and ran towards him, hugged, and kissed him. When the son began to ask for his father's forgiveness, the father wouldn't even let him finish his speech. He was so overjoyed that he commanded his servants to clothe him, put a ring in his finger, put on sandals in his feet and then called for a big feast to celebrate the return of his lost son.

Such is the joy in heaven when a lost sinner comes back to the Father in heaven -Jesus explained.

3. Good Samaritan

When Jesus taught to love one's neighbor as oneself, a certain lawyer stood up to test Jesus asking, who his 'neighbor' was. To expose the attitude of the lawyer, Jesus gave this parable. A man was attacked by bandits while traveling from Jerusalem to Jericho. The bandits who waylaid him, stripped him of his clothing, wounded him and left him half dead. As he lay there in dire straits a priest and then a Levi happened to pass by. Instead of extending help, they just passed by on the opposite side of the road. But when a Samarian came by, he showed compassion, nursed the wounded man, and carried him to the inn on his own donkey. On the next day before he departed, he left the wounded man in the care of the innkeeper and paid for his expenses.

Having told this parable Jesus asked the lawyer, "Which of the three (Priest, Levite and the Samaritan) was his 'neighbor'?" Jesus' attempt to bring out the lawyer's attitude into the open, paid off when the lawyer promptly replied, "He who showed mercy on him"- meaning that love must be shown *only to those who showed love*. To this stubborn attitude, Jesus' response was just, "Go and do likewise."

Jesus' teaching ministry contained many such unforgettable parables.

Jesus also spoke about an everlasting life which his believers will attain in the next life. He said he would give them that everlasting life for having believed that indeed he was the Son of God. This he called the kingdom of Heaven.

6.3 The coming kingdom called the everlasting life

There were and there are numerous preachers before and after Christ, teaching good morals. One of the features of Jesus' teachings that made it unique, is his teaching of a coming 'kingdom of God', which is called as the everlasting life. In fact, Jesus said that his very purpose of coming to the world is to redeem people to enable them to attain this everlasting life in their next life.

When Jesus did not hesitate to mingle among the sinners of the society, his actions were questioned. Why would a preacher who taught righteousness associate himself with such a lot? - people wondered. To this Jesus explained, "I came to call the sinners to repentance." It was God's will that sinners repent and come to him, he said.

Jesus made it plain that, at the end of our life in this world, we are going to enter an afterlife where the existence is going to last forever. Since everyone will have to face the consequences for their earthly deeds there, repenting for one's sins here, becomes imperative Jesus showed. To this he focused all his teachings. "Repent for the kingdom of God is at hand!" was the message he carried, and it was the message he commanded his disciples to carry forth. Jesus called this afterlife as both 'kingdom of God' and 'kingdom of heaven'.

Jesus said that since humankind is sinful, it is destined to everlasting hell. And God being a God of love, has sent Jesus to pay the penalty before God for the sins of the entire mankind. Thus, anyone who believes in him will have an everlasting life, Jesus said. On the contrary, if one would choose not to believe in the saving grace of the Son of God, then he proceeds as a condemned man, to ultimately end up in the everlasting hell.

Jesus quite frequently stated that he, the Son of Man (as he often referred to himself) has come to the world for the very purpose of saving mankind from the impending eternal destruction.

CHAPTER SEVEN

WHOM JESUS CLAIMED TO BE

Jesus was not only an extraordinary preacher, but he was also a unique person in many ways. He made unique claims that no other teacher or leader would ever dare to make. They are:

1. "I AM THE WAY, THE TRUTH AND LIFE"

"I am the way, the truth, and the life. No one comes to the Father except through me" Jesus said.

While there were several teachers in the wide world teaching many principles of life, instead of positioning himself as one of them or at best, the master of them all, Jesus here claims that he is the 'only way'.

By making such a claim, Jesus is ruling out the possibility of any other way to God the Father! Accepting Jesus as one of the many teachers will not be a problem at all. But accepting him as the one and only way, is entirely a different matter because if Jesus is accepted as per his claim, then one will have to reject all the others. But instead, if one must reject Jesus, then he cannot even say that Jesus is a good teacher because no sane teacher will make such a preposterous claim.

Thereby, Jesus' claim of being the only way, places the listener in a tight spot of either accepting his claim, or totally rejecting him.

2. "I AM THE BREAD OF LIFE"

Jesus claimed to be the manna from heaven. Jesus shocked the people who were following him by saying that he was the bread that had come down from heaven.

When the Israelites were brought out of Egyptian bondage by Moses, God fed them with manna from heaven. The scripture calls it the 'bread of the angels'. Quoting this event, Jesus claimed to be the bread from heaven and anyone who eats of this bread shall have everlasting life and will live forever -Jesus said. People were naturally confused. How can he claim to be the manna from heaven and how could he give his flesh for us to eat? -they wondered. As a result, many even ceased to follow him!

Before his sacrifice on the cross, Jesus gave the breaking of the bread as a sign of his sacrifice and commanded it to be done in remembrance of him. The church till date celebrates it as the 'Lord's Supper'.

It is notable that no man had ever made such a claim which Jesus had made.

3. "MY KINGDOM IS NOT OF THIS WORLD"

"Jesus proclaimed himself to be the king of the coming kingdom. He called that coming kingdom as 'Kingdom of Heaven.' This claim was the only accusation brought against Jesus before Pontius Pilate, the Roman governor.

When Pilate questioned Jesus on these charges, he said, "My kingdom is not of this world. If my kingdom were of this world, my servants would fight, so that I would not be delivered to the Jews; but now my kingdom is not from here."

Pilate therefore said to him, "Are you a king then?" To this Jesus answered, "You say rightly that I am a king."

When Jesus was crucified between two criminals, one of them called out to Jesus saying, "Lord, remember me when you come into your kingdom." Considering the fact that he was crucified and was nearing death, the reference to 'your kingdom' must be one in the future. This shows that many including the criminal on the cross believed in the claim of Jesus' coming kingdom.

And again, no man had ever made a claim of being the king of a coming kingdom. Thus, Jesus indeed was a unique preacher who ever walked on the earth.

Apart from these claims, Jesus made many "I am" claims. The following are the famous "I AM" claims of Jesus:

I am the bread of life

I am the light of the world

I am the gate

I am the good shepherd

I am the resurrection and life

I am the way the truth and life

I am the true vine

Jesus also claimed the following:

Heaven and earth will pass away, but my words will by no means pass away.

I am the resurrection and the life. He who believes in me, though he may die, he shall live. And whoever lives and believes in me shall never die.

I have power to lay it down, and I have power to take it again. This command I have received from my father.

Which of you convicts me of sin? (None had ever dared to make such a public challenge so far!)

JESUS AND GOD, THE FATHER

In relation to God the Father, there are claims of Jesus to be equal to him. Some of them are as follows:

I and my Father are one.

He who does not honor the Son does not honor the Father who sent him.

He who rejects me rejects him who sent me.

And he who sees me sees Him who sent me; He who has seen me has seen the Father

If you had known me, you would have known my Father also

THE COMING JUDGE

In the following verses Jesus promised that he would come back after his death as the judge of the world:

"For the Father judges no one, but has committed all judgment to the Son, that all should honor the Son just as they honor the Father. He who does not honor the Son does not honor the Father who sent him."

"For as the Father has life in Himself, so He has granted the Son to have life in himself, and has given him authority to execute judgment also, because he is the Son of Man."

"When the Son of Man comes in his glory, and all the holy angels with him, then he will sit on the throne of his glory. All the nations will be gathered before him, and he will separate them one from another, as a shepherd divides his sheep from the goats. And he will set the sheep on his right hand, but the goats on the left."

Since Jesus continued to make such tall claims about himself, Jews began to demand a sign from him as a proof for those claims. When the demand for a sign grew, Jesus gave them one.

7.1 The sign that Jesus provided as proof

The sign that Jesus gave them was that of Jonah the prophet. These were exact words of Jesus, "No sign will be given to it except the sign of the prophet Jonah. For as Jonah was three days and three nights in the belly of the great fish, so will the Son of Man be three days and three nights in the heart of the earth."

Jonah, an Old Testament prophet, was tossed into the sea to pacify nature's fury that arose because Jonah's action of was running away from God's will. When Jonah fell into the sea, God ordered a big fish to swallow him. Jonah remained in the belly of the fish for three days and three nights. And then when the Lord commanded, the fish spat him out onto the land.

The sign that Jesus gave thus, involved the events around his death. Jesus said that as Jonah was in the belly of the fish, for three days and three nights, he too after his death and burial, will be in the heart of the earth for three days and three nights and will then rise again alive.

If this sign will come to pass then all the claims made by him, however tall, will all be true. If not, then his claims will mean nothing.

So, it all boils down to one simple question. Did the sign of Jesus come to pass or not? Since it is the question that determines who Jesus really was, the sign that Jesus gave assumes paramount importance.

CHAPTER EIGHT

THE SUFFERING AND DEATH OF JESUS

8.1 The death of Jesus was mysterious too

As we had seen, Jesus' birth wasn't an ordinary one. Neither was his death. His death, at the young age of 33 by crucifixion was so terrible and strange that it is still talked about even today. None comprehend the awful end to a person who never meant harm to anyone.

This cruel world has a reputation for tragedies. Gautama Buddha and Mahatma Gandhi are a couple of examples among many who faced unjust ends in the history of mankind. Yet neither Buddha nor Gandhi had a clue that they were going to be poisoned or shot. Had they known, they probably would've escaped.

But this is where Jesus' death is so different from everyone else's. Jesus had definite knowledge of what awaited him in Jerusalem. He knew he was to be crucified and told his disciples many times that it was appointed for him to die that way. He knew every gruesome thing about his death and yet, he never ever attempted to avoid it. He gave in to it and embraced it wholeheartedly. It all started with the arrest in the garden of Gethsemane.

8.2 The arrest of Jesus in the garden of Gethsemane

The Jewish religious leaders wanted to kill Jesus when he came to Jerusalem for the celebration of that Passover festival. Yet, they feared a riot among the huge festival crowd in the city if an attempt was made in the open. Thus they bided their time.

An opportunity opened when Judas Iscariot - one of Jesus' disciples volunteered to betray Jesus for 30 pieces of silver. (One silver piece was a day's wage for a laborer, the payment worked out to just 30 days of laborer's wages.) Not wanting to let go a golden opportunity, the conspirators wasted no time in agreeing to his demands. They paid him and Judas assured them that he'll have Jesus in a secluded spot, well away from the crowd.

Jesus had a routine of teaching in the Temple by day and retiring to the garden of Gethsemane near the walled city of Jerusalem during the evenings. As Judas was always with Jesus, he knew where he would go.

The night of the Passover feast Jesus and all his disciples were together. It was the night Judas had decided to betray Jesus. Jesus knew very well the intentions of Judas were and told him to do what he intended, quickly; with that Judas left. No one in the room had any idea what Jesus meant. And when the feast was done, they got up and left for the Garden of Gethsemane. Jesus prayed for a while and then waited in his usual spot for his betrayer to come.

As planned, Judas came to the garden with a large crowd of people with torches, lanterns, swords, and clubs. They were accompanied by Roman soldiers and their captain. Jesus went forward to tell them that he was Jesus the Nazarene whom they were seeking; thus he gave himself up voluntarily.

It was God the Father's appointed time to hand over His Beloved Son into the hands of men, which was why they were able to lay hands on him. They had made multiple attempts before. All of which were unsuccessful until now- the appointed time.

8.3 *The trial of Jesus*

People who seized Jesus, took him to the chief priest. The other Jewish religious leaders were in attendance there. As their intention was to sentence Jesus to death, they counseled among themselves what charges may be brought upon him to justify a death sentence, but they couldn't find any. Finally, the chief priest stood up and challenged Jesus saying, "I put You under the oath by the Living God: tell us if you are the Christ, the Son of God!"

Jesus, who till now remained mute to his accusers, said, "It is as you said. Nevertheless, I say to you, hereafter you will see the Son of Man sitting at the right hand of the power and coming on the clouds of heaven." The moment Jesus uttered these words, His enemies leapt up in joy and relief. Because the claim, being the Son of God, according to them, amounted to blasphemy, and blasphemy as per Jewish laws, is punishable by death. Having thus convinced themselves of his crime, they proceeded to humiliate, beat, and spit on him.

The Passover festival brings in Jews from all over the world into the city of Jerusalem. As a result, the city becomes crowded. With such a large festive crowd in the city, the Jewish leaders knew that if they proceeded to carry out the death sentence by themselves it would cause a riot -which is sure to grab the attention of the Roman authorities. To avoid such complication, these religious leaders of the Jews decided to carry out Jesus' death sentence through the authority of the Roman governor himself.

They knew that religious accusations would not hold water in a Roman court, so they sought to bring in a political accusation against Jesus. They counseled all night long which accusation that might be and finally, before dawn, they conspired to accuse Jesus of having claimed himself to be a king. Having thus finalized their strategy, they took Jesus to the court of Pontius Pilate, the Roman governor.

There, before the Governor, the Jewish religious leaders accused Jesus of being a traitor to the Roman government.

They claimed that they found him instigating people not to pay taxes to the Roman government and instead claimed himself to be a King.

Pilate took Jesus aside and asked him if he was the king of Jews. Jesus affirmed it and said, "I am king, but my kingdom is not of this world." Pilate, from Jesus' reply, understood that He wasn't someone to instigate the people against the government. Hence, he announced to the chief priests and the crowd, "I find no fault in this man."

But the chief priests weren't going to let go that easily. They accused Jesus of stirring up people from Galilee to Judah. Upon learning that Jesus was a Galilean, Pilate found a good reason, to unburden the case on Herod the governor of Galilee, who happened to be in Jerusalem at that time.

Herod, who had heard a lot about Jesus, was overjoyed to meet him. He had a lot of questions for the famous teacher from Galilee. Jesus could have very well taken advantage of Herod's inquisitiveness. But he chose not to. He just ignored Herod's volley of questions. This infuriated Herod. So now he along with his troops began to make fun of Jesus and clothed him with a silk cloak and sent him back to Pilate.

Now, with the ball back in his court, Pilate had an easy decision before him. Not only he, yet another governor had found Jesus innocent of the charges brought before them. So, he could've just freed Jesus right away. But Pilate instead of being that straightforward in justice, began to reason with Jesus' accusers. The accusers of Jesus remained stubborn as ever and refused to budge on their demand for a death sentence.

Now Pilate had a custom of releasing a prisoner of people's choice as a gift for them during the Passover festival. At this point Pilate began toying with the idea of making Jesus that prisoner whom he could set free if people so wished. By the time Pilate brought this before the people, the Jewish religious leaders had convinced the people to ask for the release of Barabbas a convicted murderer and call for Jesus' death.

Pilate said to them, "What then shall I do with Jesus?" To this the crowd cried, "Let him be crucified!"

Now Pilate found himself cornered. He had no option but to condemn Jesus to crucifixion and free Barabbas just as the people wished. Thus, a person found innocent by not just one, but two Roman governors, was condemned to be crucified just to satisfy the mob.

8.4 *The death of Jesus*

After being thus condemned, Jesus was taken to Golgotha also called Calvary, which was just outside Jerusalem. Two criminals were also taken to be crucified along with him.

Around 9 a.m. Jesus was crucified with those criminals on either side of him. The cross was an instrument of torturous death. It is a structure consisting of an upright and transverse beam. The person to be crucified would be nailed to the cross with his hands spread wide across the plank with one nail in each hand. Then his feet would be put together and a single nail would be driven through them. After that, the whole structure will be taken to an upright position -with the person still nailed to it.

This instrument called the cross was particularly designed to inflict maximum pain and suffering in addition to death. Death never comes soon on the cross. It was common for people to suffer days-together on the cross before dying.

While on this torture instrument, Jesus prayed aloud for his tormentors saying, "Father forgive them, for they know not what they do." A little later the Roman guards present on the site, cast lots to divide the garments that Jesus had worn. Mary the mother of Jesus, was standing near the cross on which Jesus was hanging. His beloved apostle, John was also close by. Jesus looked at his mother and said, "Woman, behold your son!". Then he said to the disciple, "Behold your mother!" From that time on John took Mary as his own mother.

Since Jesus was hugely popular, a large gathering had come to witness his crucifixion. The chief priest and the Pharisees began to make fun of Jesus and his ministry, saying if he indeed were the Son of God, let him now climb down the cross, then we shall believe him, they said. The Roman soldiers standing there and even one of the criminals on the cross too joined the jeering.

As the mocking continued the second criminal on the cross rebuked the first one saying, "We deserve this justly for our deeds. But this man has done nothing wrong." Then he said to Jesus, "Lord, remember me when you come into your kingdom."

And Jesus said to him, "Assuredly, I say to you, today you will be with me in paradise."

When Jesus told him so, it was nearly 12 noon. Suddenly there was darkness all over the place for the three full hours. Darkness of this magnitude at this hour of the day was neither expected nor was comprehensible. This darkness must've bewildered both the accusers of Jesus and the executioners of the sentence equally. Jesus did not utter a single word during this period of darkness.

The chronicler, Phlegon has recorded "In the fourth year of the 202nd Olympiad, there was an extraordinary eclipse of the sun: at the sixth hour, the day was turned into dark night, so that the stars in heaven were seen."

After the end of this three-hour darkness, Jesus cried out aloud, "My God, my God, why have you forsaken me?" People around Jesus did not comprehend what he said. As they stood wondering, Jesus cried from the cross, "I thirst". At this, they filled a sponge with sour wine, (hyssop) and put it to his mouth. After taking this, Jesus said, "It is finished!". Then Jesus cried out aloud once again, "Father, I commit my spirit into Thy Hands". Saying thus, he bowed his head and died.

The moment Jesus died, the veil of the temple was torn from the top to the bottom in two; the earth quaked, and split; graves were opened; and many bodies of the saints who had died earlier were raised. The crowd who till then had been jeering and mocking the Christ on the cross, now beat their breasts and returned. When the centurion in-charge and those with him saw all this, they feared greatly and glorified God, saying, "Truly this was the Son of God!"

To confirm the death of Jesus, one of the soldiers present on the scene, pierced his side with a spear. Immediately blood and water came out. This confirmed that Jesus had indeed died.

8.5 *The burial of Jesus*

Jesus who was crucified at around 9 a.m. died six hours later at around 3 p.m. When Pontius Pilate was informed of this, he was surprised that Jesus had died so soon.

The Jews considered being crucified as a curse and a disgrace, therefore would not give those who died by crucifixion a customary burial. People who met such ends were usually buried in unmarked graves. As a result, people of such lowly death are gradually forgotten by the society and their names are no longer mentioned by the families themselves.

But when Jesus died, two prominent Jewish religious leaders came forward to conduct His burial. They did so at the risk of being chastised by their peers.

Joseph from the town of Arimathea, one of the two prominent leaders, obtained permission from Pilate to take down the body of Jesus and bury it. He then bought some fine linen, took down the body of Jesus and wrapped it in.

Nikodemus, the other prominent leader of the Jews had brought with him 45 kilograms of myrrh and aloes to be used for the ceremonial burial. Both Nikodemus and Joseph applied these to the body of Jesus then wrapped with fine linen to give it a respectful burial.

The rich among the Jews had the custom of purchasing their own burial spot. Joseph being one such, had bought a tomb for himself which was cut out of a rock. This tomb which Joseph owned was quite close to the spot where Jesus was crucified. Therefore, when they finished ritually wrapping Jesus' body, they placed it in that tomb. This tomb was a cave-like structure, a stone was rolled against the entrance of the tomb to close it.

8.6 Tomb - sealed and guarded

While alive, Jesus had expressly stated that he will rise again on the third day of his death. This was the sign that Jesus gave to prove who he was. His disciples neither understood what he said, nor did they remember these words. But the enemies of Jesus had a clear understanding of what Jesus had said. Therefore, they feared that the disciples of Jesus might stealthily hide the body of Jesus away and claim that he had risen on the third day. Anticipating this, the religious leaders approached Pilate, explaining the situation, and requesting him to seal the tomb with the Roman seal and guard it with Roman guards for the first three days.

Pilate turned them down saying they could use their temple guards if they so desired. Therefore the Jewish religious leaders themselves sealed the tomb of Jesus, and appointed guards to guard it for the first three days.

CHAPTER NINE

RESURRECTION OF JESUS

9.1 The empty tomb

On the morning of the third day, when the guards of the temple were still in place, there was a violent earthquake. An angel of God came down from heaven and rolled the stone away and then sat on it. The appearance of the angel was like lightning and his clothes were as white as snow.

At the sight of the angel, the temple guards froze in fear -so much so, they became like dead men. When they recollected themselves, they rushed to the city; some of them went and reported this to the Jewish religious leaders. This shocking news perplexed the Jewish religious leadership. A meeting was immediately convened, and the issue discussed. Having realized that their worst fears had come true, they switched to damage control mode. They summoned those guards, bribed them sufficiently, and instructed them to go around the town and spread the word that when they were asleep, the disciples of Jesus had stolen his body. The temple guards took the money and did as they were instructed.

The disciples of Jesus who neither remembered nor understood the words of their Lord regarding his resurrection on the third day, had therefore no expectations to that end. Mary Magdalene, Joanna, Mary the mother of James and Salome and a few other women came to the tomb of Jesus very early in the morning of the third day to anoint his body with spices. As they neared the tomb, they worried among themselves who would help them roll the stone away from the mouth of the tomb.

However, when they reached the tomb, they found the stone rolled away and the body of Jesus gone! As they stood frozen with surprise, Mary Magdalene turned and raced back to inform the disciples of the sudden turn of events.

To the other women who were still standing there, two angels appeared. "Do not be afraid" said one of the angels, "I know that you seek Jesus who was crucified. He is not here. For he has risen as he said." So saying, he showed them the empty tomb. The angel also reminded them of the words of Jesus whilst he was in Galilee about his impending death and resurrection. With this he asked them to go and tell the disciples thus.

Only when reminded by the angel did the women recall the words of the Lord regarding these events. They took off in a hurry to go and inform the disciples of these developments.

In the meantime, Mary Magdalene, who had reached the place where the disciples were, brought to them the shocking news of the open and empty tomb. Hearing this unbelievable news, Peter, and John raced to the tomb. By the time they reached the tomb, the other women had already left. The tomb was open just as Mary had said. Peter stepped into it and confirmed the fact for himself. Finding no logical explanation for the open and the empty tomb, Peter, and John both returned confused. But Mary remained at the tomb.

She stood there by the grave weeping. The resurrected Jesus appeared to the distraught Mary Magdalene. Mary did not recognize Jesus until he called her by her name. Then the risen Christ asked Mary to go and share the good news with the disciples. Mary immediately dashed back -this time bearing the good news.

The other women who had left long ago, had still not reached the disciples. While they were delaying and still on their way, Jesus appeared to them too. Then later Mary Magdalene caught up with them; and together they went and told this great news to the disciples. But the pessimistic disciples refused to believe the women.

However, Peter, who had just returned from the tomb, once again ran to the tomb to see for himself. There, all he could see was only the empty tomb only. He returned extremely confused.

9.2 Appearances of the resurrected Jesus

From the first day of his resurrection, Jesus appeared to many people, in various instances. On the first day, apart from appearing to Mary and the other women, Jesus appeared to two of the disciples who were on their way to a village called Emmaus. That night, when all the disciples except Thomas were assembled in a room, Jesus appeared to them all. Then eight days later, when all the disciples including Thomas were present, Jesus appeared to them once more. Thus, Jesus appeared to all of them in Jerusalem, as a risen savior.

When the disciples returned to their hometown in Galilee, Jesus appeared to them there too. There, Peter wanted to go on a fishing expedition and a few other disciples too joined him. But their all-night labor bore no fruit, and they returned empty handed. As they were returning, Jesus stood in the shore and called them to cast their net to the right hand side of the boat. When they did so, they miraculously caught 153 large fishes. At that point they identified him as the risen Lord.

When the disciples went to the mountain which Jesus had appointed to meet them, Jesus appeared to them again. This time Jesus said, "All authority has been given to me in heaven and on earth. Go therefore and make disciples of all the nations, baptizing them in the name of the Father and of the Son and of the Holy Spirit, teaching them to observe all things that I have commanded you; and lo, I am with you always, even to the end of the age."

In like manner, Jesus appeared many times to the apostles. While he was with them, he talked to them about the things pertaining to the Kingdom of God. And through many infallible proofs, Jesus presented Himself alive to them. In one instance, Jesus appeared to a crowd of more than five hundred.

When it was nearly forty days since the resurrection of Jesus, the disciples returned to Jerusalem. And Jesus appeared to them here one last time. He took the disciples to Mount Olives just outside Jerusalem and ascended to heaven right before their eyes. And a cloud received him out of their sight.

And while they looked steadfastly toward heaven as he went up, behold, two men stood by them in white apparel, said, "Men of Galilee, why do you stand gazing up into heaven? This same Jesus, who was taken up from you into heaven, will so come in like manner as you saw him go into heaven."

CHAPTER TEN

THE IMPORTANCE OF JESUS

Everything we had seen thus far, are historical happenings that had happened nearly two millennia ago. A lot has happened since then. To say that the whole world has changed since, cannot be an understatement. When that is the case, how can an event that happened in such a distant past, affect us, who live in an ultra-modern world?

We now know that Jesus' life- his birth, his ministry, his death, and his resurrection was miraculous. But it's his claim to be the Son of God that sets Him apart.

It was exactly because of this claim, that the chief priests and scribes found him guilty of the death penalty. Yes, the Jews killed him only because Jesus claimed to be the Son of God, thus claimed to be equal to God. The only sign that Jesus gave as a proof of who he was, was that 'He would die and rise up again on the third day.'

The question now is, "Did he rise again, like he said?"

Well, though it's been two thousand years since the death of Jesus, the tomb in which he was buried remains empty and open still - to this day in Jerusalem.

10.1 Why is the tomb empty?

The fact that the tomb of Jesus is empty, demands a logical explanation; one way or the other. Many had of course tried to explain the empty tomb phenomenon over the ages. The very first explanation given was what the foes of Jesus gave as soon as they came to know that the tomb was empty - *that the disciples of Jesus had removed the body of Jesus stealthily and then proclaimed that Jesus had risen from the dead.*

First, it must be noted that the disciple did not stand to gain anything by claiming so. In fact, by claiming so, every disciple lost whatever he had. They even had to undergo persecution and die horrible deaths just for making that one claim. One may be prepared to die for the truth or what he believed to be the truth. But no one willingly face death, that too by torture to something he knows to be untrue. This testifies to the claim of the apostles that Jesus Christ had indeed raised from the dead.

That the apostles had gone to another tomb by mistake and made a claim that Jesus had risen is another explanation put forward. This statement does not hold water because, if the disciples of Christ had gone to the wrong tomb and made that absurd claim, then all the foes would have to do to shut down the claim was go to the right tomb, and bring the dead body of Jesus to be paraded in the streets of Jerusalem and not persecute the disciples -this, actually they did!

Some others said *that the tomb is empty because Jesus did not actually die on the cross. He only swooned in it. The Roman soldiers made a mistake and they buried Jesus alive. Since Jesus was buried with a lot of myrrh and aloes- which had medicinal effects, he was revived, and he recovered enough to come out of the grave.*

Firstly, the Roman soldiers who declared that Jesus was dead, were no ordinary people. They were professionals who had enough experience in carrying out crucifixions. One of them had in fact, confirmed the death by piercing the side of Jesus with his spear.

Secondly, Jesus, who had been beaten and ill-treated throughout the night, was hung from the cross for nearly three hours before he died. Even if he has just swooned and not died, being entombed with nearly 45 kilos of myrrh and aloes alone will be enough to kill him: as that amount of fragrance is more likely to knock a perfectly healthy individual unconscious -And not recover!

Thirdly, even if the recovery of a swooned Jesus is granted, he had three challenges before him. First, despite his weak state, he must muster enough strength to roll away the stone from the mouth of the tomb and second, somehow scare away the guards posted there. Third and the most impossible task would be to convince his followers enough to motivate them

to die saying that Jesus has indeed risen from the dead. Since none of these are even remotely possible, we can easily rule out the swoon theory.

Finally, there was one theory proposed to explain the empty tomb. The proponents of this theory proposed that Jesus being the Son of God, was taken from this earth by God, before men could lay hands on him. And in his place Judas the traitor was allowed to be crucified.

This theory explains Jesus being alive but not the empty tomb! Where did the body of Judas go then? Secondly, even if everyone mistook Judas to be Jesus, Judas himself could not have mistaken thus, and would have made every attempt to avoid such a death. He certainly would never have cried to heaven for the forgiveness of his tormentors!

Hence, the only plausible explanation for the empty tomb is the fact that Jesus had indeed risen as he had said on the third day. The empty tomb stands as a testimony of this fact for the last two thousand years.

10.2 If Jesus had indeed risen from the dead . . .

Rising from the dead on the third day was the only sign that Jesus had given as proof that he is the 'Son of God'. Since the empty tomb of Jesus testifies that he had indeed risen from the dead on the third day just as he had said, it stands as a proof that Jesus **is the 'Son of God'** *just as he had claimed to be!*

As the Son of God cannot lie, all that Jesus had said and claimed during his lifetime will become the truth revealed from God Himself.

The things Jesus had said about: sin and its consequence of eternal damnation; the life after death; everlasting life called the Kingdom of God where the righteous go, all these become facts to be trusted because, he proved that he really is who he said he was.

Jesus described both heaven and hell as real places gave a graphic description of each of them, while most people think them to be just a figment one's of imagination. Of the place called hell, Jesus said that it was a place God had prepared not for men but the fallen angels. But those who chose to serve the devil, God condemns them along with the devil. It is a place where the fire is not quenched, the worms there never die, and it is a place which is covered in darkness – where there is weeping and gnashing of teeth.

The fact that the tomb of Jesus stands open and empty puts paid to speculation can heaven, hell afterlife could all be just a figment of one's imagination. The empty open tomb of Jesus brings them all into the realm of believable truth.

We are now here on earth. At one point of time in the past, we did not exist; now we do; and there will come a day when we pass away and we will be on this earth no more. Since the resurrection of Jesus is the conformity that 'afterlife' 'heaven' and 'hell' are very real, it is imperative for us to take a serious look at the 2000-year-old event of resurrection of Jesus.

10.3 The incredible prophecies that were fulfilled in Jesus

A prophecy foretells the events of the future. A prophecy coming true is an incredible thing. At the same time one could also wonder if it could be a coincidence? For example, if someone tells a pregnant woman that she would give birth to a son and the lady indeed does give birth to a son, everyone will naturally think that it could well be a coincidence.

But if someone, five years before the girl is even married, foretells the exact date and time at which she is going to deliver her first baby and the gender of the baby and if that comes to pass exactly as foretold, and then there can be no question of coincidence, as the probability of such precision is almost nil.

Prophets have been foretelling the events in the life of Jesus, for centuries. The number of prophecies were not just a few but more than 300! The following are some of them, and the number of years before they were told:

1. Genesis 3:15 (4000 years ago) – The Savior who will come as the seed of the woman shall bruise Satan's head (The salvation Jesus earned through the cross).
2. Micah 5:2 (700 years before) – Messiah will be born in Bethlehem (Luke 2: 1-7).
3. Isaiah 7:14 (700 years before) - Messiah will be born of a virgin (Matthew 1:18-21).
4. Isaiah 40:3 (700 years before) – The one who prepares the way will come before Him (Matthew 3:1-3).
5. Zachariah 9:9 (500 years before) – Messiah will come riding the colt (Mathew 21:6-11).
6. Psalms 41:9 (1000 years before) – Messiah will be betrayed by one who is very close (Mathew 26:49, 50).
7. Zachariah 11:12 (500 years before) – The rate to be agreed to betray the Messiah (Mathew 26:15).
8. Zachariah 11:13 (500 years before) – The payment made for the betrayal of the Messiah will be used to purchase a potter's land.
9. Isaiah 53:7 (700 years before) – Messiah will hold his peace before his tormentors (Mathew 27:12).
10. Psalms 22:16 (1000 years before) – Messiah's hands and feet will be pierced with nails (Luke 22:33).

The possibility factor of a foretold event coming to pass is explained as below:

If one detail is foretold, then the probability of that one detail coming true will have a probability of 2 in 1, that is

50%. (If birth of a baby is foretold, there are two chances namely, either a baby will be born, or no baby is born)

If two details are foretold, the possibility of those two details coming true will have a probability of 3 in 1. The possibility comes down to 33%. (If birth of a baby and its gender is foretold, there are three chances namely, either a baby will be born or no baby is born, and if the baby is born, it may or may not be of the correct gender).

Likewise, as the number of foretold details increase, the possibility of it fully coming true dwindles tremendously as seen below:

If three details are given the possibility becomes 8 in 1 (12.5%)

If four details are given then possibility becomes 1 in 16 (6.25%)

If five details are given the possibility is just 1 in 32 (3.125%)

If ten details are given the possibility goes down to 1 in 1021 (0.09765625%)

The chances of just eight of the above mentioned ten prophecies coming true in a one human is worked out as 10^{17} that is 1 in 100,000,000,000,000,000 possibilities. There are more than 300 prophecies foretold about Jesus. The possibility for just 48 of them coming true in one man has been worked out to be 10^{157} that is 10,000,000,000,000,000,000,000,000,000,000,000,000,000,000, 000,000,000,000,000,000,000,000,000,000,000,000,000,000,000, 000,000,000,000,000,000,000,000,000,000,000,000,000,000,000, 000,000,000,000,000,000,000,000!

In that case, one can see the absolute impossibility of all 324 prophecies foretold about Jesus happening in his life just as they were foretold! **But every single one of them happened as they were foretold!**

Therefore, along with the empty tomb of Jesus these completed prophecies too stand as a testimony of who Jesus truly is. He was no ordinary man. He is **the Son of God**.

10.4 *The heavenly life that can be gained through Jesus*

Jesus said that God the Father had sent him, the Son of God, to the world so that the world might be saved through Him. He even said that he had come to offer his life as the ransom for the salvation of the world. John the Baptist who introduced Jesus to the world introduced him as the 'Lamb of God' who takes away the sins of the world. He did not come into this world to live an exemplary life or teach morals or to deliver the afflicted. His only purpose was to take away the sins of the world.

We have all sinned, none of us can say that we haven't, and God is a just God. And because He is a just God, He punishes sinners. Punishment for the wrongdoer is called justice. When this punishment is fulfilled, the wrong deed is nullified. Instead of being punished, the wrongdoer cannot satisfy justice by doing a lot of good. Nor can he make it good by going on a pilgrimage or doing penance or something similar.

In God's eyes, every sin should be paid for by the blood. This is the only price that God accepts for sin and nothing else because that is how serious He views sin.

Since we cannot bear to pay the price for our sins, Jesus shed his sinless blood to satisfy the justice of God; so that the actual sinner (you & me) may be innocent before God. In other words, Jesus paid the price that the justice of the Holy God demanded and earned our salvation.

Jesus accomplished it by his death and crucifixion. He was sinless when he was condemned to die. Pontius Pilate who judged him found him innocent. Herod Antipas, another Roman governor before whom Jesus was brought also did not find any guilt. Even the centurion who was tasked to crucify Jesus testified that he indeed was the Son of God.

Jesus said that his blood that was to be shed is the new covenant, which is shed for many for the remission of sins. Jesus was sent forth as propitiation to this world by God so that the whole world may not ultimately end up in the eternal damnation of hell but could be saved through faith in the sacrifice that Jesus made by shedding his blameless blood.

That is why Jesus said that He was **'THE' WAY,** and none can go to the Father but through Him. Jesus' blood has been given as a propitiation for our sins. This offer by God is not made to be applied to all irrespective of one's willingness, but it is for only those who are willing to take this offer of God. If we accept this propitiation, it will apply to us. By taking up this offer of remission of sins through the blood of Jesus Christ, we can head towards an eternal life with God forever. This is called **SALVATION** from sin.

Jesus put it thus, "No one has ascended to heaven but he who came down from heaven, that is, the Son of Man who is in heaven. And as Moses lifted up the serpent in the wilderness, even so must the Son of Man be lifted up;that whoever believes in him should not perish but have eternal life. For God so loved the world that He gave His only begotten Son, that whoever believes in him should not perish but have everlasting life.For God did not send His Son into the world to condemn the world, but that the world through him might be saved."

Jesus invites everyone to accept this salvation He offers saying, "Come to me, all you who labor and are heavy laden, and I will give you rest."

10.5 How can I be saved by Christ?

How to be saved through Christ? How to receive the propitiation of one's sins?

First, one has to recognize that he/she is a sinner in need of salvation. When we talk about sin, many think that very deplorable acts as murder, rape or burglary are sins. In the sight of the Holy God, the smallest act or intent or even the thought that is not right before Him is sin. In light of that fact, we must realize that none of us are perfect and everyone is a 'sinner' in the sight of God.

Every sinner is poised to face the wrath of the Holy God, since His justice demands it. As a result, the whole of humanity is doomed to be condemned to hell by God's righteousness. But when we appropriate the forgiveness earned in the eyes of God by the blood of Christ, for our sins, our sins are washed clean, and we are found righteous in the name of the Savior Jesus Christ.

Hence, upon the realization that I am a sinner bound to go to hell, one must turn to Jesus and confess our sins before him and ask for forgiveness for our sins; request to be cleansed by his soul cleansing blood, thus be included with those saved by him. When one realizes his sin and confesses and asks for forgiveness, Jesus immediately forgives him and washes him off all his stains of sins thus making that person pure and holy in the eyes of the Holy God.

Salvation through Jesus is thus **free and easy to obtain**. No penance demanded; no pilgrimage commanded. Anyone can obtain it. **IT IS FREE OF COST AND AVAILABLE TO ALL**.

If you are yet to experience this salvation from your sins, please realize that Christ died for your sins too. He does not wish you to enter the eternal damnation of hell. For a sinner to escape God's wrath, he took God's wrath upon his sinless self. If you just request him for that forgiveness from sin, he is willing to give it to you.

Turn to Jesus today. Confess your sins and ask for his forgiveness. He will cleanse and make you whole.

May the Lord bless you.